The RavenMagick Crow Cawnicles

The Magick
of the Mother Tree

Volume One

Written by Catherine Blackwood Hollister

Illustrations by Lucas Boyd Wallenfels

Dedicated to

THE MOTHER TREE
&
THE RAVEN PEOPLE

THE RAVEN PEOPLE

There is a Glint in their Eye,
A Knowing.
A Sparkle to their Beingness
One cannot deny.
They are the Raven People.

The Raven People
Own their Magick,
Wear it like a Diamond Crown.
With Pixy dust,
They spread to all they encounter,
On Wings of Enchantment.

They are a Curious sort,
Always Questioning,
Never completely satisfied…
They have X-ray vision,
Seeing deeply into one's Being,
Asking for Truth.

Raven People live for the Sparkle in Life,
The Shiny objects.
They hop from one to the next,
Collecting for their Treasure Trove…
Sharing with those who Understand.

They have a Deep Wisdom,
Often misunderstood, potentially feared.
Their message is direct… with no apologies.
They are confident in their delivery,
Asking for nothing in return.

The Raven People are here to be heard;
They have an Ancient Knowledge
The World needs Now.
Listen to their Message;
See beyond the Veil.

Discover the Magick you will find here…

ETERNAL RIVER OF RAVEN MAGICK

The river she flows, day in and day out, never pausing for anything that disrupts her flow.
She always finds a way… in, around, through, and over.
She is on her own journey.
Present and Flowing.
Gravity pulling her forward, to her destination, she complies willingly.
The joy and freedom of flow she embodies with every drop of her being.
The steep walls that hold her give her direction she does not question.
She just moves, in the most natural way, devoted to the journey.

INTRODUCTION TO THE CROW CAWNICLES

Welcome to the Magical Mystery Tour
Back to Self.
May these Writings Spark
A Remembrance in You.
May they Feel Familiar.
May they Ignite your Soul and
Inspire you Forward,
As they have for me.

I have written myself through my life,
The Words Gifted to me.
Each Day searching deeply
Into the corners of my Soul.
Clearing the cobwebs and Deconstructing
All that does not Serve Me.
May this be the same for You.

Nature has always been my Guide;
She is the Truth.
I have learned from her Ways
How to Be in the World.
She has taught me with such
Patience and Grace,
And for that I am Grateful.

May these Writings bring you closer to Nature
And her Gifts.
May she show you the Way back to the Earth,
With your feet Deeply Rooted in her Rich Soil,
So that you may Grow new Roots
And new Shoots.

These Writings are simply to Inspire you
As they did me.
Show you a way Through a Confusing World
With their Simplicity.
Show you the way Through
And Back to Yourself.

All my Love,
RavenMagick

WRITINGS

1. LET NATURE BE MY GUIDE

Here we go.
The Beginning of the Mystery…

Where do I start?
How will I know?

Listen.
Nature will Guide you.

Nature always knows;
She never misleads.
She is Honest and Forthright,
Guiding with consequences…
All in our best interest.

If we Listen, Watch, and Learn,
She will tell us the ways of Life.
For she is the Exemplar,
Showing us the way
Back to our Nature.

So Listen I will,
Learn from the Metaphors,
Learn from being in my Nature.
Following her Lead
One step at a time.
Back to myself… over and over.

Let the Journey begin anew;
May her Mysteries be revealed,
Leading us All forward
Back to our Nature.

2. INSPIRED BY THE NIGHT OWL

The Night Owl is always Present
Even in her silent flight.
I can hear her Wings
Move through the Night Sky,
Stealth and Sure,
Showing me the Way.

She travels into the Dark;
I follow…
With an X-ray Vision,
She sees through illusion,
Knowing what is real.

The Night Owl sees in all Directions,
Hears the unheard.
She is Wise, she is Potent,
Clear with her Message.
She Leads and I follow.

I Honor her Guidance,
Grateful to learn her Ways.
She shows me what I cannot see:
Revealing the Gems that were always there,
Removing the Veil,
So I may see clearly.

The Night Owl is my Guide,
For that I am Grateful…
I will become One with her,
Learn her Magick,
Know the way.

3. THE LAND WHISPERS

The Land is Whispering…
"It is time."
Crystalizing right alongside of us,
Each realizing a New Way of Being.

One with the Land,
We will Grow together towards
A new Future,
New Possibilities.
Listening, Collaborating, Creating…
For the Benefit of All.

We are the Stewards of this Land,
It is the Steward of Us.
An Energetic Reciprocity.
We are not separate
But one Driving Force.

A Creative Force
This World has been waiting for.
The Land will Lead us,
Whispering its Requests
So that we may Follow,
Grow together,
Creating an Unimaginable Future,
One we never thought Possible.

It is time.

Listen… deeply.

4. DANCING WITH THE ELEMENTS

As I dove deep into the dark-blue
Mediterranean Waters,
I Remembered we were Water.
As I felt the warmth of the Sun on the
Rocky Mountain Cliffs,
I Remembered we were Stone.
As our Flames danced together in
Vibrant red, orange, and yellow,
I Remembered we were Fire.
As we blew like Leaves through the Midnight
Sky,
I Remembered we were Air.

We are One…
With All.
We have always been All.
I am you, you are me,
We are Nature in its
Ever expansive expression.

We are the Hawks overhead
Who have landed here.
We are the Owls nestled together
In the branches of the Ponderosa.
Shape-shifters…
Taking form as we see each other
Through the other's eyes.

Cleaning up loose ends,
Finishing the edges,
So that we may step forward
In Step…
Leaving the Past where it stands,
Moving forward with the Present
Into the Magnificent Future.

You are the Protector;
I am the Protected.
We Belong Here,
With an ever-watchful eye…
Preening each other's Feathers
As we Fly with the Gift of Freedom.

Our Love knows no bounds,
For we are the Nature that surrounds us.
We are the Elements…
We are the Spark that ignites the Fire
Within our Soul.

5. NATURE'S BALANCE

Nature holds the Balance;
She is the Exemplar,
The Truth.

Looking closely,
Nature shows us how to Live,
To be Present.
How to soak up the Sun and Rain,
Both necessary for Survival.

She shows us how to Live from one Season
To the next,
Transforming as needed.
Our Roots holding us Strong,
Allowing us to Grow…
Or sleep.

Nature teaches us how we are all
Connected…
Each a piece of the puzzle,
All Valuable and Necessary.
She shows us Balance,
And the Harmony that comes from that…
The Ease and Grace of it All.

I Watch her and Listen for clues:
How to be a better Human,
To appreciate Beauty in the small things
And the Magnificent.
How to Be.

To find Balance and Wholeness,
Appreciate the Perfection of Imperfection.
She teaches me about Stillness…
The Peace it reveals.

Nature brings me back to Myself
Over and over again.
Showing me I am part of Her,
She is part of Me,
We are One and the Same.

Nature is my teacher;
I am hers.
The instruction manual,
Is right before our eyes.
The Example of a Balanced, Whole Life
And how to Live it
Is right outside our door…
Waiting for us to See.

6. GIFT OF THE STORM

I sit within the calm,
Sun shining on my face,
Noticing the thunder clouds in the distance
As they come my way.
The Storm is inevitable.

The warmth and quiet feel so good…
I soak it up.
It doesn't challenge or provoke me;
I am held and comforted within its Grace,
And for this I am Grateful.

As the Storm builds,
I wake from my slumber.
It is inescapable.
I must Lean in, Face it…
Prepare for the challenges to come.

This Vessel I have built
Over a Lifetime,
I have learned to Trust.
It holds me strong within the Storm,
Anchors me…
Showing me the way Through.

Though at times I get blown over,
My tools strewn across the landscape.
I cannot find them in the Storm.
Confused and Disoriented,
I lose my way…
And I don't have the answers.

I question all that I thought to be true;
I doubt all that I have learned.
Who am I really?
I am lost for a moment in time,
Wondering how to find my way again.

In the moment I feel I will be lost forever,
The Storm settles…
I can see clearly enough to gather my tools,
Noticing they have been cleansed and
Sharpened by the Storm.
The Sun peeks through the Clouds,
And I Begin another Day.

7. WAVE RIDING

This life requires skill.
It requires us to pay attention,
Learn the rules,
Hone our abilities,
Sharpen our sword,
Have a strategy for how we move.

Life is this big beautiful Ocean,
Encompassing us All,
Asking us to Learn her Ways.
To Swim in her Depths
As she holds us,
Showing us the Way.
For She is the Mother of All.

We ride her Waves…
Sometimes with a Grace and Ease that fills
Our Soul with such Joy and Reverence.
We Trust our skill; We Know how.
She allows us to Merge with her.
We Connect with ourselves in this moment,
Knowing this is the Way.
We are Held, Supported, Loved.
A Brilliance to Behold.

Then, as a Mother does,
She tests our skill.
She sends in the Big Set…
The Waves are Enormous.
We frantically try to swim to shore,

Out-swim the Power of Fear,
Which looms behind us.
But it catches us… as it is faster.
We get pummeled, twisted and turned,
Confused and disoriented.
We are asked to Surrender to what is.
She takes us,
Imposing her Strength and Will,
Until she is finished with the Lesson.

Somehow we come up for Air,
Finding Gratitude for our next Breath…
There is no Time to tend to our Wounds,
So we prepare for the next bigger Wave.
She says, "Turn around,
Lean in and Face your Fear… "
We must trust her Guidance,
So we turn towards the Wall of Water
Before us.

It is all we can see;
There is no out-swimming it this time…
The only Way is Through her Depths:
To Dive Deep into the Roots of this
Wave of Emotion,
Embody the Serenity that comes with
This Commitment…
And the Peace these Depths Behold.

8. MAGICK OF THE MOTHER TREE

I sit beneath her Branches with
Immense Gratitude
For All that she Is and All that I Am.
She is the Anchor,
The Embodiment of Ancient Magick,
Her form Dancing with the Wind,
For All to witness.

She calls me to her daily
For conversation and company.
She is so Wise in her Ways.
Sharing freely her Love,
Support, and Guidance…
Bathing me in her Grace.

I can count on her to Be There,
To Be Here:
In my Heart, Always.
Whether I am near or far,
Her presence warms my soul.

Her Roots are my Roots,
Her Branches twist and turn…
As do mine.
She Dances in the silence,
To music only she can hear…
As do I.

I choose this Magnificent Tree
As my Mother:
She birthed me to be All that I Am.
I will care for her as she cares for me…
We are Committed to each other,
In this Life, And Always.

May this Prayer Honor
her Existence,
And Mine.

9. LOVE'S EXPRESSION

To be loved…
Completely.
Held with such Reverence,
Honored so deeply…
Fills my Heart to the brim.

To be Seen,
Understood, and Appreciated,
Loved so dearly…
Is beyond the walls with which I lived.
This kind of Love is beyond
The Gates of Heaven.

Nature has always held me
In a way I understood.
We had an agreement to take care of
Each other…
Our Love Simple and Pure,
Honest and Forthright.

She taught me her Ways.
How to Love.
How to Feel.
To Give and Receive
From a place of reciprocity.
To fill myself up completely
From my own Energy and hers.

I had to learn Love
To know Love.
I had to be the Beacon that called it in,
The signal Strong and Bright,
Confident and Sure,
For it to find me.

I can say now…
I have found the Love that I longed for.
It came to my door when I wasn't looking,
When I was ready to receive it,
Nestling its sweetness into my Life.

10. FLIGHT OF THE MAGPIE

Magick brought her to me,
Laid her at my feet
With Reverence and Grace.
She was not long for the World,
So I held her and sang her
To the other side.

Her Radiance was Magnificent:
Colors of the Rainbow
Glistening off her Feathers
As she prepared herself
For the Transition.
Her last Flight from here to there…
A Place we can only imagine.

She was a Gift
Sent with a Message.
I Listened as she took her last Breaths,
Knowing there was an exchange happening,
Hoping to hear the Message.

She Blessed me with her Magick,
Reminding me I have Wings…
To use them.
She showed me how we Transform,
From the Physical to the Ethereal,
And that it is All the same.

She told me to Express my Creativity.
Freely.
I can not do it wrong.
"Let it Fly," she said…
Let it Fly.

So I will let her Wisdom take Flight
Within my Heart and Soul.
I will hold her Gift
With Sacred Hands…
Knowing I have been Blessed by
Her willingness to die.

11. MIGRATION TO THE FUTURE

As I Wake,
There on the pond are Seven Geese
Welcoming me into my Day.
Bathing, Preening, and Honking
With outstretched Wings…
Knowing they are Safe.

There is a Message,
Always…
I will not let it Fly by.
What do they Represent in my Life?
At this Time,
What are they telling me?

I am Safe.
I am Supported.
I am Free to rest when needed,
Take Flight when Urged.
My Flock is Guiding and Supporting me as
We Fly forward together.

The Future is calling,
The Migration inevitable…
In my Bones and Blood,
I Listen to the call from within,
Knowing the way without having to Know.

We will Fly great distances together,
Protect and Support each other…
Through Storms, Wind, and Rain,
We will Persevere,
Answering the Call.

Love, Trust, and Loyalty
Band us together,
Keeping us Strong.
Following our Purpose
Forward to a place we know we have been.

12. MY MOTHER IN HER GARDEN

When I think of my Mother,
I see her in her Garden,
Diligently tending to her Beloveds.
Hand watering and caring for each with the
Brush of an Artist.

Completely in the Moment.
Hour by hour,
Day by day,
She supports each Plant with Love.
Tending to their branches,
Clearing debris,
Helping them Grow
Into the most beautiful aspect of
Themselves…
As she Grows into Hers.

She watches them Thrive
With Tenderness and Joy,
The Reciprocity of Nature filling her Soul
With all the nutrients she needs…
Completing her.

I think of the Commitment this takes,
Each and Every Day.
The Strength, Will, and Determination
To keep showing up for Herself,

Her Garden,
And the Planet.
This One Act is all it takes to shift a
World in Chaos
Into a World Renewing Itself.
The Planet we all came here to experience.

Such simplicity…
Overlooked and underappreciated.

She leads the Way,
Tending to her Garden,
Tending to Herself,
Tending to the Vibration that shifts all of
Nature and Humanity.

She is the Exemplar,
Showing the Way Through in her
Quiet Determination.
Let us Honor this Simple yet Powerful
Way of how to be in the World.

My Mother in her Garden brings
Joy to my Heart,
Comfort to my Soul.
I have so much Gratitude for
Being a Flower in this Garden…

13. THE WIND

Here she comes…
Such a Force,
I can't help but to notice her.

She is the great Disrupter,
Creator of Chaos and Confusion.
As I Witness her Power,
I hold Steadfast in my Center,
Willing her to blow over and above me.

I Fear her Fury and wonder why…
I want to Tame her,
Turn her back into a soft breeze,
Make her Disappear.

Why can't I let her be
The Cleanser that she is,
The Wild Force that makes us Stop,
Creatrix in Action?

Can I welcome her Fury?
Allow her to be however she needs to be?
Remaining unchanged by her Presence?
Can I let her blow over,
Through, and around,
Celebrating her Wildness,
Chaos, and Disruption?

The Wind will be who she needs to be;
She is the Wind of Change,
The Cleanser of the Earth…
She is the Example to us All
How to unapologetically be
Wild and Free…

14. EYE OF THE TEMPEST

How do we Stay in the Eye of the Storm,
This calm, centered place,
When the Winds of Trauma and
Fire of expression surround us?
How do we stay in the Stillness,
Remaining Sovereign to the
Call of our own Voice?

The Storm wants to take us:
Whip us up in her violent torrent,
Feed on our Soul,
Make us doubt our Sovereignty,
Question our Serenity.
The Chaos so compelling we are drawn to its
Lightning Energy,
Forgetting we have a choice
Not to engage with her Force.

Quiet.
Sit in the Quiet.
The Peace.
The Tranquility of Self.
Let the Storm brew and blow as she will
In all her Glory,
In all her Fierceness.

Honor the Storm;
Allow her to be there,
Remembering there is a Choice…
To be taken by her Force,
Whipped up by her Wildness…
Or Stand Solidly in Sovereignty,
Trusting in the Peace and Calm of the
Eye of the Soul.
Allowing her Blow by to another Day.

15. QUIET WHISPERS

As I Wake to the still Snow falling,
Tree branches a frozen masterpiece,
The landscape draped in a
Soft blanket of white,
All I hear is…
Quiet Whispers.

Nature rests in this Stillness,
Bathing herself with Silence.
She does not resist
Nor try to outrun it
But Surrenders to what is,
Content in her Hibernation.

And yet I am Restless.
I want to Move, Do, Accomplish…
Get ahead of "it."
I don't know why…
I just can't comply.

My Body says rest.
My Mind says go.
My Spirit says listen… deeply.
I am Paralyzed in a state of Confusion,
Not able to hear a Sound.

And there, just there…
Is the Key hiding in the darkness.
Listen for the Silence;
Let it speak its soft voice,
Tell you what matters most.
Let this Stillness bathe you in her Wisdom.

May the Quiet Whispers Guide me;
May Nature remind me to
Change with the Seasons,
To Embrace what Is,
To Surrender to my Soul,
Trusting it knows the Way.

16. MAGICK AND THE BABY HAWK

There she sits, Hawk by her side.
She has delivered this Gift
With such Reverence and Tenderness.
Senses alert to all Dimensions,
Magick sees what I can not see.

My Heart breaks for this little Life given,
This Sacrifice of Flight.
One less Hawk to fill the Sky above me…
The Wisdom that comes with this Gift
Is not missed:

I give my Life for you
To receive this Message.
The Giving and Receiving of Life,
The Sharing of Wisdom,
From Above, Below, and all Directions,
The Sacredness of Life in all its forms…
Honor this and know you are
Held in the highest.

Receiving this sacred Gift
With Gratitude and Honor,
I take her delicate little form
With Magick by my side.

We Honor her brief stay on
this Earth,
Her Dedication to this Life, and the
Sacredness of it All.
I send her with a Blessing back
To where she came from…
Knowing she will
Fly with me still.

17. THE PATHWAY HOME

As I walk with my Four Leggeds
In the soft morning Light,
I Breathe in the fresh crisp Air,
Greeting the Trees, Sky, and Clouds…
Letting my feet fall softly on the Earth.

I take this Path every morning…
And sometimes I don't.
Each Day is different.
One step at a time,
I fall into the Rhythm of the
Energy that Leads me.

I can't do this wrong,
And I can't do this right.
There is no wrong or right that
Guides me.
I just Listen, and then step…
Waiting for my feet to touch the ground
Towards my next Experience.

There is so much relief
Not having to do "it" right,
A Freedom that fills my lungs with Air.
I Celebrate each step I take,
Excited for the unexpected Gifts
Laid before me along the Path.

Sometimes I trip,
Sometimes I fall…
But the Ground is always there to catch me,
With her warm Embrace,
Dusting me off,
Encouraging me Forward.

Each Day the Path is different,
As there are many to choose from.
To know they are all
Paths that lead me Home
Brings me Solace,
And I can Breathe again.

Catherine Blackwood Hollister, *RavenMagick - author*

This is the first volume of writings Cate has published, though she has played with words and expression throughout her life. Her childhood into adulthood on the land inspired her to speak through nature, to use nature as an advocate, a guiding force through life's twists and turns. These words have been gifted to her from a source unknown, yet a close confidant and ally.

Lucas Boyd Wallenfels, *Illustrations using DALL-E*

Lucas, Cate's youngest, has spent his youth expressing himself through his creativity. This collaboration was a perfect match for the two to come together. These are his first published works, matching the writings beautifully.